ACQUIRED COMMUNITY

I

~

I LOVE A PARADE

A BRIEF HISTORY OF SODOMITES: SOME CLASSICAL FACTS

That homos were cool then, from Homer to the fall of Rome.
That the Ancient Romans were okay with gay, as long as it was with a slave.

That on red-figure vases from Classic Antiquity, Eros appears only with boys.
That on black figure cups, the courting erastes holds the boy's gaze,
reaches down to sexually stimulate, the Up and Down gesture is plain.

That Alcibiades was the first known transgendered "fix" by Christian scholars.
That *he* was turned into a *she* famed for her beauty,
lest it be written that Socrates had a gay lover.

That Alexander the Great had a great love for men and women.
That he fasted and had flutes banned, had horses manes and tails shorn,
when he mourned his divine hero, his soul mate, Hephaestion.

That the Spartan male-warrior ideal
included intimate male bonding,
thought to enhance their brotherhood in battle.
That the Sacred Bands of Thebes was an all-lover regiment,
and one hundred, fifty pairs had to be annihilated
refusing to surrender.
That this might serve the NHL, the Navy Seals.

That Ovid wrote *A boy's love appealed to me less*
and Medieval moralists changed it to *A boy's love appealed to me not at all.*
That one is more poetic.

That Hadrian had a lover, the legendary beauty, Antinous,
whose face was used by Raphael when painting angels.
That Hadrian's Wall could've marked the length of his mourning
over his lover's premature death.

That some still blame the fall of the Roman Empire on homosexuality,
not the unsustainability of a slave economy,
nor the Barbarians,
nor the rise of Christianity,
nor the Byzantine riches from trade routes and spices,
nor Constantinople's greed for diverting taxes.

That a modern-day Catholic scholar,
defending the fight against gay marriage,
refers to Rome's homosexuality and tells us the real danger—
that we return to Pagan sexual morality.

That if Christianity is crumbling like Hadrian's Wall,
re-use the stones to construct new dwellings.

MARCH ON WASHINGTON, 1993

What struck me first was the sheer numbers, queers everywhere.
Battalions of sailors and infantry, proud in their uniforms.
Eventually, I made uneasy peace with this equal right.

And merchandise galore—I got a Keith Haring t-shirt before he was cool.
ACT UP wore their Silence=Death shirts, staged mock funerals.
Cybill Shepherd gave a pithy speech, her presence enough,
a heterosexual woman willing to stand, out of one hundred movie stars asked.
Martina Navratilova—
her journey from behind the Iron Curtain, to tolerance in tennis,
to finally belonging, among a million people, on the Mall.
The Indigo Girls, still in the closet, claimed ally status.
Six hours of entertainment peppered with speeches promoting equality and coming out.
Nancy Pelosi read the President's message to cheers and boos.
We were where it mattered, not in a colony, not watching on TV.

It was queer central in Dupont Circle,
antiques, boutiques, sex toy emporiums, bookstores.
Dykes ate on the cheap: falafels and pizza,
while the men saved their scant caloric intakes for haute cuisine.
Later we all drank in the same bars.

The men congregated near the Washington Monument.
I expected a condom to be rolled over that giant phallus.
Near the White House, which seemed unoccupied, lay The Quilt—
coffin-sized panels sewn together, football fields long.
We sobbed as did most everyone else.

In New York state, driving home
small-town papers diminished the event
to a few queens and scantily-clad men,
gave equal press to the coterie of Bible-thumpers
with their futile attempts at shaming and conversion.
When our van-load of dykes crossed the border
we breathed a sigh.
The Globe and Mail reported a million people at the March.

Back then, there was still hope that Clinton would act on his promises.
I was learning to be outraged.

THE LAVENDER SCARE

According to a concerned mother of a Women's Army Corps recruit,
Fort Oglethorpe was full of homosexual sex maniacs in WWII,
"women having the appearance of perverts have been observed—
mannish haircuts, clothing, posture, stride...
seeking to date other girls, paying all the bills."

—from "Coming Out Under Fire"

Only if we were "addicted to the practice", could we be discharged in wartime.
It was a gay time, the war.
The General ignored all our signals—
      we whistled that ode to secret lovers, the Hawaiian War Chant,
      said, "We're going to have a gay time tonight"
      or "Are you in the mood?"
The Inspector General ignored civilians
cruising servicemen along highways near bases,
the bars we frequented, men in drag, women arm in arm.

Ignored, that is, until peacetime,
when, addicts after all, we were given blue discharges.

The Lavender Scare rendered us
      shunned from civilian jobs,
      ineligible for GI benefits,
      unable to go back to small towns and family farms.
Some of us moved to D.C., L.A., SanFran,
      some started homophile groups,
      some men got married but fucked other men in the bushes,
      some women became stone butches and never let their lovers touch them,
      some of us jumped from tall buildings.

SMASHED UP LINES FROM A STONE BUTCH
(found lines from Leslie Feinberg's *Stone Butch Blues*)

There were two kinds of fights in the bars—
one between butches—full of booze and shame,
and one with our real enemies—
drunken gangs, Klan-type thugs, sociopaths and cops.

The next time the cell door opens it will be me they drag out and chain,
spread-eagled to the bars.
You prayed you wouldn't hear me scream.
I didn't.

We had to be wearing three pieces of women's clothing.
Rolled up our sleeves, slicked back our hair in order to live through it.

Tammy was singing "Stand By Your Man," and we were changing all the he's to she's.

The cops picked out the most stone butch of them all.
They stripped her, slow, in front of everyone in the bar.
Later she hung herself.

Outside, you loosened my tie. Fingers light on my shoulders, you said,
"I'll never get these stains out."

Did it hurt you the times I couldn't let you touch me?

In a glance you'd memorize the wounds on my body like a road map—
The gashes, bruises, cigarette burns.

You treated my stone-self as a wound that needed loving healing.
No one's ever done that since.

We embraced the word *gay*, thought we were liberated
until they called us chauvinist pigs, the enemy.

Then I began passing as a man.

THE NATURE OF ARGUMENTS BETWEEN CLOSETED COUPLES

Circle which number applies, 1-strongly disagree, 5-strongly agree

It bothers me to see two homosexual people together in public 1 2 3 4 5

We fought over gradations of tolerance. I was willing to walk if more than 100,000 people were there, Tess refused to attend at all in case her mother finds out, though in the end she watched from the perimeter. At least she came to the parade.

Gay people make me nervous 1 2 3 4 5

Whether there should even be a dyke march (she said no) and I didn't go the first year.

I avoid gay individuals 1 2 3 4 5

Whether to sign her on to my health benefits—she claimed she wanted to pay for her own dental. Tenants in common vs. joint tenants when we bought our home.

I fear homosexual persons will make advances towards me 1 2 3 4 5

I request benefits anyway. The HR advisor did up the top button of her blouse. I wanted to disappear, when the younger assistant entered and said she'd be happy to check into it, asked how *my friend* was and didn't we just move in down the road from her. The nerve of that old hose bag, in her polyester frills and tight perm, assuming I'd want her. I couldn't tell Tess any of this—she'd be mad that I asked.

Homosexuals are immoral 1 2 3 4 5

Trying to be cool, we agree to an "open relationship," but the fierceness of first love doesn't withstand the messiness of someone else and who wouldn't want to escape into the tanned arms of an HR assistant, while her husband was away.

I have damaged the property of a gay person such as "keying" their car 1 2 3 4 5

And now I see how it unravelled—who the hell fights about those things in that television world we grow up believing? The one where dads go off to their jobs and moms lord over the garden and groceries until it's time for their soap. Maybe they fight about what he doesn't do: take out the trash or babysit once in a while.

I would feel uncomfortable having a gay roommate 1 2 3 4 5

Finally, each of us alone in a dim rented room with only the echo of "gay relationships don't last as long; they lack commitment, they all sleep around."

Gay people deserve what they get 1 2 3 4 5

The house foreclosed. Neither of us could carry it alone.

*italicized text from a homophobia questionnaire in *Victory Deferred: How AIDS Changed Gay Life in America.*

FINDING WHERE THE WOMEN WENT, 1965

The tuxedo set would escort their drag queens
into the back of the King Edward Hotel
on New Year's Eve, while news cameras rolled.

Women were left to search for rundown juke joints of their own.
Cil called Information, but got nowhere.
Instead, she and her girl hailed cabs on Yonge Street,
asked them where the women went.
Most cabbies refused until a sympathetic one
drove them to the Continental, by the bus terminal,
guarded by a tattooed butch, who said,
You want the office types, up at the Parkside
when Cil asked if the Continental served mixed drinks.
It turned out they wanted a dive above the army surplus store, Hercules, on Yonge.
They asked two women smoking a joint outside
where the bar might be, were escorted to an unmarked door.
Sarah the owner, from Mobile, Alabama, admitted them grudgingly.

They danced until someone cut in,
whom Cil thought fancied her.
Instead the man-woman asked,
Which one of you is the butch?
They both stared blankly.
Next time one of you needs a haircut.

Cil and her dates complied, for another ten years,
in the dives that passed for clubs: The Cameo, The Blue Jay, The Quest,
until women were allowed to look like women.

"THE ANITA BRYANT"

This was no Selma, no Stonewall.
Still some stood up, boycotted Florida orange juice,
after Anita, the bouffant beauty queen of Oklahoma,
poster child for Christ and orange juice,
waged her campaign.

Gay bartenders across America replaced "Screwdrivers" with "the Anita Bryant,"
made from vodka and apple juice,
and gave the proceeds to gay rights groups
after Anita said, *They recruit children because they can't have their own* and
Next we'll have to give rights to prostitutes and to people who sleep with St. Bernards
and to nail biters.
Her Save Our Children campaign repealed equal rights laws in Miami-Dade
for thirty years.

God made homosexuals and Anita Bryant.
Homosexuals made "The Anita Bryant".

Anita unmade herself—
lost the orange juice job, her marriage,
(which she blamed on gays)
left a trail of unpaid employees,
and declared bankruptcy in Arkansas, Tennessee and Missouri.

A day without orange juice.

THE CLIT CLUB, CIRCA 1991

We gawked at Go-Go dancers on the dingy stage,
strip-teasing at a lesbian bar.
The locals yelled *cunt* like it wasn't a bad word.
Why would these women dance for women?
Surely not for the tips.
Disgusted and enthralled, my friends and I
folded a bill into a cleavage or two,
guffawed.

Now what.

A subscription to
On Our Backs or
Off Our Backs,
S&M or feminism—
who knew the difference?

After a couple of drinks, we toured the backroom
complete with a pillory and trapeze
before we donned our college jackets,
squinted our way into a Manhattan afternoon
of hawked wares and lonely drunks,
used clothing displayed on dirty concrete,
and proselytizing madmen from their curb pulpits.

We sought cheap draft and falafels,
discounted poetry
in lightly soiled hardcovers,
souvenirs for our mothers.

GAY BASHING

Show me a queer that hasn't been bashed in one form or another
sometimes by family, sometimes a stranger.

Once, late at night on the Bloor viaduct walking home hand in hand
yelled at by men and terrified they'd circle round in their car again.

Once with our twins in their car-seats as we neared home.
A man yelled "fucking dykes," his kids looking on.

After my letter to the paper reminding progressives not to be smug,
we became the Nelson confessional for tales of bashing thugs.

A crone has missing teeth—the ex-husband came over,
tire iron in hand after she left him for her female lover.

The cops refused to charge my hair stylists' basher with a hate crime,
what's a straight boy to do when they came on to him.

Or the trans-woman wielding pepper spray,
finally in her own body, learns she too, is prey.

Once by my own brother, no twice,
though the time he only yelled is almost forgotten.

Show me a queer that hasn't been bashed, in one form or another.
sometimes by a stranger, sometimes a brother.

LESBIAN NUNS: BREAKING THE SILENCE

Lesbian Nuns, purchased at Coles, on my third attempt, in this Catholic town.
Grainy pictures of up-tight nuns, or kindly ones who've been turfed-out.
Tales of pained love, kissing each other in the convent's dark,
praying together for release from sin, head nuns who hit them with sticks.

Paperback wedged in my dorm closet,
after my daily den-mother duties—
unless there's some emergency, then, stuffed under the bed.
I fear I'll leave the contraband behind, when my donship is done.

The book is my escape, as are twice-weekly badminton games
with older women who may or may not be gay.
They come in pairs; I linger near.
One pair invites me to a party at their ninth floor condo,
Chianti and brie for twelve women, overlooking the river and lit-up locks.
I sink into a leather couch, answer questions about school and work.
Restraint electrifies the air; I long to ask how they came out.
Without a car and transit stopped—the College too far to walk—
Jennifer says I can sleep in *her room* and she'll bunk with Jill.

I lay awake accompanied by a crack of light from the guest bathroom,
I'm gay gleaming on the tip of my tongue, as possibilities explode in my heart,
that there are others like me, that I may live a fulfilled life on a ninth floor,
and the light refracts through some shiny glass art object
scattering beams across the breadth of my worry.

Mid-morning back at the dorm,
Bert, stinking of Molson and Drum, professes his love.
Erin talks about her dad hitting her mom.
Nancy asks why I didn't come home.
I dole out advice as a twenty-year-old can,
dissociate while fly-boys and foresters call each other fag.

Long train journey home, break my silence,
angst-ridden confession, through the safety of Canada Post.
The badminton players write back,
we would have come out to you first, but we had too much to lose.

PRELUDE TO THE SHRINERS

Kingston, visiting my parents
on the same weekend as the first annual Pride parade.
Sixty Queen's students and some political dykes,
we walked down Princess Street
half-smiling, on-guard for attacks; verbal or otherwise,
worried we'd be seen,
something in us wanting to be seen.

By the end, crowds lined the streets.
Purple-fezzed middle-aged men with rather large girths
driving mini-motorbikes or clown-cars followed the last of us.

Purple fezzes—but we were the freaks.
The crowd, I convinced myself, was for us.
Memory, being what it is,
imprinted "Gay Shriners" into bystanders' minds.

There was a gay picnic afterwards
but no Shriners came.

WHAT LESBIANS WEAR TO THE MALL

A phys-ed teacher in Belleville, Ontario who can't come out,
invites me to do a lesbian "show and tell" in health class.
The girls are quiet but fidgety while she introduces me,
a picture of normal—chinos, pastel cardigan, Birkenstocks.
Portray a boring life that is anything but:
just bought our first house, sailing, walking my dog,
on the verge of joint health benefits, mostly out.

One of them asks when I knew. "In university," I reply.
Strictly true but crafted so they wouldn't get scared,
no mention of how knowing unfolds—

I was electrified in high school health class,
but high school is so fucked up,
what we most want to know, we can't ask.
I broke up with a decent guy to hang with girls,
quelled my doubt by having sex with young men.
I hung on by a filament, it took years to comprehend.

One student asks, "What do lesbians wear to the mall?"
It was the pinnacle of lesbian-fashion-meets-mainstream,
when Birkenstocks were "in."
I chuckle but dare not say, "I wouldn't know."
I joke, "Birkenstocks" and they all look down,
some tuck their feet beneath their chair.

A girl at the back perches at a spare desk,
freshly scrubbed longing,
she begged the teacher to sit in on this class.
I peg her most likely
to stay afterwards.
She dashes off quickly, as I had dashed from Grade 10 health class
with Ms. Broadbear, total geek and, in retrospect, a dyke,
in her tinted glasses and baby-blue sweat suit,
pre-Birkenstock frumpy black sandals,
tentatively taught a lesson on "h-o-m-o-s-e-x-u-a-l-i-t-y"—
decriminalized in 1969, delisted as a psychiatric disorder 1974,
described the male sex act,
with no reference to what women did—apparently, not much.

Ms. Broadbear's demeanor pleaded not to be asked,
but I ached to know if she was one, and if so, did she find love.

The room was silent until the bell.

PEELER BAR

I'd never met a dyke until Gina
hired me, her underling,
my first lesbian fling.

Tattoos on her knuckles, leathery face,
she ran a sheltered workshop.
Gina had a soft spot for a guy whose body was burned head to toe.
Bad enough he was born a retard, she said, *then he was scorched.*
She took him for drives on her days off.

Gina liquid-lunched at the peeler bar on Fridays.
I asked my dad if he wanted to go,
I heard they had good, cheap lunches, I said.
He was game.

Jail guards frequented the smoke-choked bar for decades,
limestone spawn across from the Kingston Pen,
kitty-corner to the Prison for Women.
The gyre on stage—
the worn, the new, the long-legged, the bleached,
wearing clothes I'd never seen,
whirly gigged tits, bikinis in a bar, quick-release pants.

My boss was alone at a table near the stage;
the waitress greeted her with a draft and a nod.
Gina smoked while she watched the show.
Our eyes met, she flung me a cheeky smile
with those gleaming false teeth.
Did she lose hers in a bar fight?

My dad and I ordered lunch,
Blue on tap, the fish 'n chips predictable.
Afterwards, he dropped me off at the sheltered workshop
and I said, "that was strange."
"Yeah, didn't think you were the type."

NOTHING TO FORGIVE

Home from college for the holidays
facing my parents in the living room,
I say, *I'm gay*—
I couldn't bear to use the "L-word."
My parents respond, *we love you,*
but little else.

Fears unrealized.
I weep that night.

For months we talk only about
work and school, winter sports.
Much later my mother says,
It was our problem to get over, not yours.

WEIGHT OF THE EMPIRE

Sod off.
When grandma scoffed *dirty sod*
I thought *earth,* but I noticed contempt.
Bugger—*you little bugger,* my father always said
with the weight-of-the-Empire-behind-him smirk.

Linguists claim that *sod-off* and *bugger-me-sideways* are just slang terms,
divorced from their origins,
benign and diffuse.
In jolly old England, *Getting the little buggers to behave* is a curriculum teaching tool.

In my health class, the boys saved their squirm for sodomy,
though, in the dark, you could be cocksure
they'd penetrate anything they could.

I was electrified by *homosexual* and its euphemism *gay,*
relieved *dyke* wasn't the object of titter,
yet I knew to make my urges disappear until freshman year.

But what about my brother?
All the hallmarks: sensitive, a procession of fag hags from an early age,
prancing round the playroom to *Gloria,* in love with boy bands.
As a teenager, he refused to swim in our pool without t-shirt and shorts,
he never came out directly despite me paving the way.
Our father guessed he was gay, asked over Skype from 6000 miles away.
He visits for a week a year, bewitched by the fantasy of his model family,
complete with gay-bashing brother.

My bugger-brother hides in the folds of his flesh
on the other side of the world
in a country never colonized by Britain,
where the etymology of bugger is irrelevant,
closeted at work and dancing in gay bars
that proliferate around the US military base
because DADT means those American sods can dance and sweat,
can love in the dingy, drunken shadows,
between roll calls in homophobia's empire.

Sod off—
a minced oath,
cuts its roots to gay sex
as sure as *gosh* to God
as sure as *blankety blank* to fuck.

As benign as *Paki*,
grandma's contorted face, dad's smirk,
twist their way through our DNA.

COMMITTEE OF ADJUSTMENT

In '87 forty dykes showed up,
in heels and hose
with the City of Toronto planners,
for the Women's Common rezoning hearing,
so they could get a liquor license—
their own place to dance and eat,
that wasn't run by men,
or the mafia—
a sort of dyke "Legion,"
the first of its kind anywhere.

"Drag" took on a new meaning that night.
The dolled-up dykes did the trick.
The committee adjusted.

FIERCE, NOT SILENT, NIGHT

Who ever heard of a bustling church these days,
but Christmas Eve, the Metropolitan Community Church
fills two services at Roy Thompson Hall

with queer hordes, there by choice,
not childhood obligation,
some even ducking out on their families to pray gay.

So many wept and were grateful,
rediscovering what had been taken away,
seen for their humanity

in a church that accepted them once and for all.
Agnostic or not,
I knew that I too, belonged that night.

I could finally hear the *compassion* message,
not blood of Christ, nor virgins
and what the hell is myrrh anyway.

Fierce, not silent, night,
1000 strong we held strangers and prayed,
sang and swayed in the grand hall.

SECOND OBITUARIES

Is this what Michael Lynch meant when he urged us to "make dying gay?"

The dailies in large cities
got used to running second obituaries,
when the parents had gone home
to Timmins, or Blenheim or Napanee,
gutted with compound grief
after they buried their sons—
in services presided over by clergy who were paid to scrub
the word gay from a very gay life.

Surrounded by a circle of friends, Peter succumbed to pneumocystis carinii pneumonia
after a courageous fight with AIDS. Peter founded AIDS ACTION NOW and
performed, up until last month, in his beloved weekly drag show at Chaps.
He is survived by his lover, Daniel, his best friend, Kate and his dedicated music students.

instead of

Our beloved son Peter, high school soccer star [a.k.a Straight],
teacher and soccer coach, survived by his sister
and his parents, died suddenly at thirty-six.

Obliterate the last decade, expunge the word "estranged" from family
and an announcement of death looks conventional
until, reading enough of them,
you realize there was an epidemic of men dying,
whose lives were not worthy of mention
once they left home at eighteen, their middle age.

CELEBRATION WAS A SIDE EFFECT, 1992

From my thirtieth floor cubicle,
tears obscured my view
while the rainbow flag was hung
on the gay community centre.
But the excitement at Pink-Turf soccer,
followed by a Pride brunch at friends'
was what put me over the edge.

I decided to go,

despite a blow-out with my girlfriend the night before.
She could only bear to watch from a bank tower at Yonge and Bloor,
for fear her mother would find out.

Long before politicians clamoured to march,
let alone sign proclamations,
I was skeptical that a parade could take over downtown.
My fear soon defused when tens of thousands ventured out,
despite a few protesters with *Abomination* placards and
cops gritting their teeth at having to work,
though a peaceful crowd meant easy overtime pay.

Glamour boys mingled on fancy balconies,
strung with pink triangle streamers
and raised their martinis in the clear air,
feeling no need to be counted amongst the crowd.
Not an inch to spare on The Steps as bears and leathermen vied for prime real estate.
Straight-looking men with camo pants and tight jaws lingered on the parade route,
but nothing came of their menace, though I was not the likely target.

Political dykes with banners distanced themselves
from the muscle boys in their tighty-whiteys atop dance club floats.
The PFLAG banner made me cry while I walked with them,
wishing that someday my parents, too, would march.
Worry that the gay church crowd would break out into *We Shall Overcome*
kept me moving.
I found the float with the best dance music,
just ahead of Totally Naked Toronto—a few older naked men,
their flaccid presence less threatening than the leather dykes up ahead.

Midway up Yonge, near closed doors—Church of Scientology and House of Lords,
an Asian man in a corner store, who barely spoke English, greeted me with a smile.
He could attest to the economic benefits of the parade,
knowing full well Sundays are usually dead.
With a line up behind me, I'd bought his last bottle of water.
I wanted to stay and watch the parade but made my way outside,
alone through the sidewalk crowds of those afraid to march.
Behind the Toronto People With AIDS float—
red ribbons, emaciated men,
I was thankful for the relief of Fruit Cocktail's antics—
Carmen Miranda and her fruity hat.

It's impossible to know if a man is dying, when he's all dolled up like that.

Through bottlenecked crowds on Church, I thought
this mob would be easy for police to disperse
with leftover tear gas from the bathhouse raids,
or what if a man gunned his Camaro through the hordes?
I found the Pride stage,
watched Carol Pope grind and sneer, to the crowd's delight
and eyed cute women who were uninhibited enough to dance.

Drunk on warm draft at the beer garden and
relief that the day was safe,
I walked to the College streetcar.
Smirks from passengers didn't escalate
but a triangle wedged in my gut, far too *out* in my Pride t-shirt.
I berated myself for not bringing a change of clothes.

In my shared house, empty that night,
threat of violence was an uneasy bedfellow.
I needed a lover and victory sex,
but instead watched the Pride recap on CityTV
and marvelled at the day.

II

KEEN

Michael Lynch was a scholar, poet and activist. He helped found the AIDS Committee of Toronto, Gay Fathers of Toronto, the AIDS Memorial and the Toronto Centre for Lesbian and Gay Studies. At the time of his death, he was writing two books, *The Age of Adhesiveness* about male-to-male intimacy and a biography of Walt Whitman.

AFTER MICHAEL LYNCH'S *THESE WAVES OF DYING FRIENDS*

The book is at the Toronto Reference Library—
white ribbons of floors around grand stairs,
open space and security guards.

1.6 million volumes, five floors of books, and Michael's is in the stacks.
The apogee of my search, this thin collection of activism and mourning.
I've come 3000 miles to read this out-of-print elegy.

Written by a professor, founding father of ACT,
early warning signal against panic, dad,
before he succumbed at 46.

It feels like I have the last one.
With each page I turn, the sheets fall in my hands—
gone brittle, the glue does not hold.

To preserve the pages, I need Michael's famous yellow kitchen gloves,
used for mocking the police, similarly gloved, at AIDS protests
We want you all beside us on these steps, this other dance floor, gloved fists in the air

but no, they're more apt for activism and I sit here.
Give me archivist gloves instead.
What if he were still alive. What if they all were?

He was wrong when he said,
Leave eloquence to those who haven't lost their first half dozen friends,
Michael, I need both pairs of gloves now.

SIGHTINGS

Ceaselessly musing, venturing, throwing, seeking the spheres to connect them,
Till the bridge you will need be form'd, till the ductile anchor hold,
Till the gossamer thread you fling catch somewhere, O my soul.

—from *A Noiseless Patient Spider* by Walt Whitman

I lingered in the bushes,
my name on the third pillar.
Michael Lynch, died, 1991.

You, Chad, rippling blonde,
getting off with a young beefcake
just before dawn, in Cawthra Park.

I smiled at your muscular enthusiasm,
the way you insisted on a condom,
non-negotiable. And to think that I used to

rail against condoms, circle jerks,
armpit licking as a substitute for rimming,
any curb of our sexual freedom.

The way you sauntered off, afterwards,
presumably to study,
as if you had all the time in the world,

but I saw my book,"These Waves of Dying Friends"
peeking out of your satchel.
If only I'd finished the Whitman biography.

I am the one with the immortal smile, watching.
My skin, cyanotic blue, but perfectly intact
from all the touching and care as I neared the end.

OUR BODIES WANT LIFE, OUR HISTORY REVENGE

This isn't a séance, it's my life.
I don't want to talk with you, dead guy.

> *I proceed for all who are or have been young men,*
> *to tell the secret of my nights and days,*
> *to celebrate the need of comrades.*

Whether you quote Whitman or not,
I'm not your comrade.

> You remind me of my younger self.
> I'm keen to help you study my work.
> You'd get better grades.

Maybe so but,
I don't want you watching me go down on a guy.

> But you are in a park.

Yeah, but you're dead.

> Come on, it's all I've got.
> I haven't felt this in decades,
> hot from sex, not night sweats.

You would be an old man now, seventy,
gone soft,
a permanent fixture at Fire Island.
What do you need with sex?

> *I sing the body electric!*
> My ghost-body still wants life.
> Right-wingers tried to wipe us out.
> I celebrate your torrid sex.

MORE SEX

For the one I love most lay sleeping by me under the same cover in the cool night,
in the stillness in the autumn moonbeams his face was inclined toward me,
And his arm lay lightly around my breast —and that night I was happy.

—from *When I Heard At the Close of Day* by Walt Whitman

Chad sprawls on a bench in Cawthra Park,
in the dark,
arched back,
getting blown,
then fucked,
by a man he found on *Grindr*.

When they're through, he looks towards the hedgerow;
he can just make out the pillars of the AIDS memorial,
though not the names.

After sex, he doesn't want to think about Michael Lynch.
His name on the third pillar, 1991, the one with three hundred others.
The names continue their upward incline for five more years
until the limited miracle of AZT
was mixed in a cocktail,
shaken.

Chad wants only to feel tingle of groin, spent cock
re-live the thrusts of the Adonis he picked up,
immortal as sin, shoulders like a beam,
Affliction jeans tangled round his perfect shins.

When he steadies his legs, Chad walks into an all night diner,
for bacon and eggs.
He's not thinking of gay marriage rights—
that was won when he was ten.
He's not thinking of safe sex, that's all he knows.
Nor of killing himself, living wills,
nor stench, contagion, rage,
not worried about dying from AIDS.
His lesbian and gay studies scholarship affords him this meal.

He wonders what Michael would say,
perhaps his rally cry: *more sex, better sex, safe sex!*
But Michael is long dead.

GIVE MY LOVE TO SOCHI

Michael,
I'm monitoring the Sochi Olympics
for anti-gay discrimination,
through Human Rights Watch.

> Ha, you complain about me watching you!
> I will leave you alone, but Russia won't.

It's over the internet.
They can find other gay-rights observers
on the ground.

> Either way, you aren't free.

Why are we still here?
Isn't your sacrifice enough—
and then Matthew Shepard,
or kids killing themselves?

> Stop feeling sorry for yourself.
> Write and study and fuck those
> who want you in the restroom
> before they return to their wives.
> Linger at the baths,
> make the mainstream howl.
> Go to Sochi
> with my yellow kitchen gloves.

Yeah, gloves'll help me in the gulag.

> They might…
> when you're fisting another convict.

I prefer my activism online.

Putin doesn't care about petitions,
neither does Coca-Cola.
Rainbow-drape a tank,
drive it through Sochi
during the opening ceremonies.

Why not the Kremlin?
Where the fuck will I get a tank?
I'll send postcards instead,
fuck an Olympian.
I'll tattoo *gay is good* on his chest.

You and Johnny Weir,
staying safe at home,
allegedly to focus on careers.
Do you think we cared about protecting our jobs
when we were part-time pall bearers
in middle age?

I'm tired of your lectures.
Thanks for all you've done
but it's different now.
I don't have to march in the streets.

Yes, because we marched
and kissed in the streets.

Maybe humans just evolved.

It's revolution not evolution.
I understand why the feminists were so upset.
Why the coat hanger and "Never Again."

My mother has that sticker.
It's barbaric.

You entitled prick.
If I was alive, I'd cuff you,
then write a long piece in the *Body Politic.*

The *Body Politic* no longer exists.

"Evolution" takes many generations,
enough gay men got gassed
along with the Jews.
None of us should let
marching in the streets go.

Sorry, sorry.
I just want to move forward.

Ah, *the world only spins forward*—
"Angels in America" was written long ago,
We **are** citizens.
You need angels and a map
to see where you've been
or you will walk in circles
proclaiming everything new.

Seeing the world as if for the first time—
wonder is good.

So is talking about genocide.

GLORY

I onward go, I stop,
With hinged knees and steady hand to dress wounds,
I am firm with each, the pangs are sharp yet unavoidable,
One turns to me his appealing eyes—poor boy! I never knew you,
Yet I think I could not refuse this moment to die for you, if that would save you.

—from *The Wound Dresser* by Walt Whitman

Michael and his friends went to war movies,
when they were well enough.
They wept for the savage loss of those youthful bodies in *Glory.*

Their civil war fought on legislature floors and drug company doorsteps,
as throngs of men died off and were replaced
by new ones who didn't yet know they were infected.

Michael brought pentamidine across the border,
prolonged lives, because his government refused—
political will replaced by lassitude.

The AIDS Memorial was built in the thick of loss,
by those who'd yet to die,
to help others in their mourning,

a community of grief
where once there was only silence.
Not a war memorial.

In the Civil War,
more people died of infection
than battle.

TRANSFIGURATION

Tell me, when you dance,
do you rage against loss?

Huh? No, we just dance
in the hopes of getting laid.

A good thing, I guess.
After each funeral,
we brought them back to life between us,
radiant upon a dance floor,
forgetting the mournful mime
that we supposed a death dance.
Vigorous rout, electrified our bodies.

Leave the vigorous romp
to the bathroom, the park, the bedroom.

Rout, not romp. Look it up.
And I'm talking transfiguration.
Your dead friends' liveliest gifts—
their energy, longing, rage.

Magic, like in Harry Potter?
Alteration of form,
A bird into a goblet?

No.
The Gospels.

What?

Jesus, radiant upon a mountain—
shining with bright rays of light.

Come on, really,
you compare dead friends to Jesus?

What point is there to all those gospels,
if not so that we see ourselves?

What point is there to religion?

The greater good.
I grew up Protestant and glad I did.
Religion gave me stories
and a place to put my rage.

Yeah, all those churches really stepped up
during the epidemic.
What do you think happens after we die?

I'm a ghost.
No pallid mourning.
Just furious rage on the dance floor
that electrifies our bodies with energy,
transfers power to the living—
that could only have been his legacy.

Whose?

Another dead friend.
A new Jesus.

Careful, you'll go to your hell for that.

Wait, you are telling me to be reverent?
All your sex and fluid ethics,
your post-AIDS privilege.

Ah, your soapbox.
Stand down.
It's just dumb luck.

Do you think only Jesus shines with rays of light?
Do you think your energy comes from only you?

I thought...

Not by yourself, you didn't.

NO SHAME

Chad can almost hear Michael pleading with gay men
to eradicate the readiness of guilt,
encourage them to make dying gay.
But what about living?
Does Chad need to be a dad to be complete?
Fuck his way through the whole community?
Does he have to be a perfect role model,
in that twisted way homophobia works?
Overachievers, all of them.
Michael's obit longer than his life.

Fuck the yellow kitchen glove,
the death, contagion and rage.
By luck of birth, he's got the Charter of Rights
and no shame.

BLUE HARVEST

I haven't seen you around in a while.

In paths untrodden there by myself
away from the clack of the world.

Ah, comrade,
you've discovered Whitman.

I'm working at a lumber mill for the summer,
helping with the lodgepole pine harvest.

You and Whitman in a mill town.
Where?

Northern BC,
monoculture of trees.
They upped the harvest
once they learned the blue wood is sound.

Blue Wood?
I'd be blue working there.

Pine beetle fungal spores
stain the sapwood blue.
It's not so bad, working here.
I pass.

"Passing" doesn't sound like much fun.
I hope you get to Vancouver on weekends.

I see some action here.
Closeted hard bodies
who work the line and have wives.

Do you wear a condom?

Of course.

                                                                Where do you meet?

In the forest.
In the grey spindles of limbs and
red pine boughs, none are still green.

                                                                My last years,
                                                        I planted a blue garden—
                                                        salvia, spires of larkspur,
                                                                geraniums, vetch.
                                                My nurse wheeled me to find blue plants.
                                                        My doctor brought me seeds,
                                                        that's all they could do pre-AZT.

Scientists pry open the bark
with little knives,
paint individual trees with a salve,
avoid pointing fingers of blame.
It's not yet cocktail hour here,
just red death.

                                                                We were the hub of blame.
                                                Men's deaths got plotted on a colour-coded map
                                                with a Post-it note from the Minister of Health
                                                        that said over the lavender epicenter
                                                                "burn in hell."

18 million hectares of trees
apt to burn
and no blame—
monoculture,
climate change,
clear cuts.

36 million deaths to AIDS—
we were blamed
until it moved beyond
the gays.

Lodgepole pine cull,
how many board feet of lumber,
blue pine boxes.
The lumber mills dormant
until the next reforestation
reaps its slow benefits,
by then whole communities in ruins.

My blue garden, that last year—
the centaur retired, salvia long-blooming,
blue geraniums flourished still.
Decayed spires of larkspur refused to be mourned.
So many names—
genus and species.
They all shall not die in vain—
Pinus contorta,
lobelia, geraniums, vetch
Rupert, Craig, Callum.

Michael, might you have chosen a burial,
blue wood for your pine box,
beetles clinging to the lobelia
to hasten your decay?

Blue.
I would.

ELEGY

Song of the bleeding throat,
Death's outlet song of life, (for well dear brother I know,
If thou wast not granted to sing thou would'st surely die.)

—from *When Lilacs Last in the Dooryard Bloom'd* by Walt Whitman

For class, I had to read,
"When Lilacs Last in the Dooryard Bloom'd."

Didn't you think it a masterpiece—
from mourning to acceptance of death?

Wordy and beautiful.
But I'm tired of reading elegy.
I want to read about the living.

You should be so lucky.
I mourned and yet shall mourn
with every returning spring.

Do you talk to others,
where you are?

As a ghost? No, just the living.
But I miss friendship—
bonding and bondage.

Is it hell?

I spent my last eight years
burying my friends and
organizing my own death.
This is enjoyable, talking to you.

Why were you so into Whitman?

I'm American and I'm gay.
I love the erotic fraternity.
His were poems of praise not shame.
Pre-homo/hetero dichotomy.

There have always been gays:
the Sacred Band of Thebes,
150 pairs of lovers—
elite force, heroic.

I guess that has romantic appeal
but they weren't called "gay."
There have always been homosexual acts.

Yeah, in jails and war.

Some men need war.
Or sport.

Even Whitman changed his pronouns
to feign heterosexual love
and fiercely denied
his romantic love for men.

Go back and read "Calamus,"
look up images of the plant
on that hand-held device.
Better yet, tramp round a pond,
tell me what you see in the tall grass,
his choice of calamus is not incidental.
After his lover Kapos died,
grief-stricken Kalamos drowned too,
then turned into reed,
his rustling in the wind a lament.

There is just so much veiled love
and lament.

Believe in the power of metaphor.
Use your imagination.
Don't judge your mentors too harshly.

I just wished he'd say sweet fag instead
of all the riffing on sweet flag.

There were no sweet fags;
the notion didn't exist.

How could fags not exist?

Think of Whitman's time as the
pink-tinged roots of our community
but no real community to speak of then.
That must have been hell.

I love the gay community.
Our community.

What have you done to help our community?
We forged our own families of choice,
created bonds of affection not blood,
celebrated sex, helped each other die.

But I don't want to keen,
I want to live.

                                        So did we.
                        If you want immortality, write a book.

Your book falls apart in my hands.

                                Read others, including elegies.

Damn the elegy.
It took decades for all of us to plainly say
I love you to someone who is alive.

                                        Eventually, you will love
                                more of the dead than the living.

III

~

OUT OF THE BLUE

BRAVE

Surging down pavement on the side of Morning Mountain,
25mm of rubber keeps me safe at fifty km/h.
I think *I'm brave*, and then almost lose my nerve,
fingers hover over brake hoods, while I steel myself.

Waves of dying men care for one another knowing they too will succumb.
Dozens of memorials a year and still their hearts open, no brakes on.
After work, choose to visit the AIDS ward,
instead of going for a drink at the bar.
Choose to love with no cure.

Since when do young men ask: *what entitles me to friends who grow old?*
Everyone dies and many have died young. Who am I to wish for better?"
Since when do *immortal* young men need courage?

They start to in 1982.

The road is cracked,
shadows obscure pocks,
so I whistle down the middle,
hoping that cars will wait,
as I careen around a corner,
pedal home along the ridge.
Brave—no—
just deluded that I'm safe.

Thirty years on, should I die riding my bike,
some would still shake their heads at the stupidity
of relying on thin rubber to preserve life.

ST PATRICK'S DAY PARADE 2014, BOSTON

Letter from the Massachusetts LGBT Vets to the South Boston Allied War Veteran's Council,
"We write first and foremost to reject allegations that we do not exist."

Danny boy, you better not be a fag
or a smoke bomb will come your way;
we'll let you march if you are a vet
as long as you hide that you're gay.

Danny boy, you better not want peace
because we've banned Veterans For Peace from the parade.

Danny boy, you better not drink Guinness at the pub,
for Guinness won't sponsor us anymore.

Danny boy, you better not be a politician;
they refuse to march in our private parade.

Danny boy, you better go back to Ireland;
the gays march openly there.

ACQUIRED COMMUNITY

Tried to ignore the cologne of alley sex and stale draft,
bullies in muscle cars come to bash gay heads,
bewildered men pushing their dying lovers down Church Street,
no closer to Lourdes at journey's end.
I hoped only for safe passage from the gay ghetto to a bed
where we'd make it up in the forgiving dark.

AIDS quarantine was on state ballots. My friends joined ACT UP.
Our emaciated brothers made their final voyage for D.C. not Fire Island,
lobbied anyone who'd listen, despite knowing they'd be long dead.
The aggrieved sewed a quilt bigger than the Mall.
Lesbians donated blood, served on hospice boards.

Mark Doty held Wally—
they were all holding someone—
while I lived Bidart's lines—
forever is coming out—
or not. Or not. Or not. Or not. Or not.

Would dykes be next? Thrilling first girl-kisses laced with politics and death,
which I only learned to taste when I saw *The Normal Heart* off-Broadway,
noticed bumper stickers: *love>hate,* marched on Washington.

Some lost hundreds of comrades. A purple lesion was death.
Heads spinning, their own T-cell counts tanked.
Some drug trials killed every man, yet more volunteered en masse.
Cashmere and candlelight, freesia adorned the wards.
Men donated their eyes.
A hundred thousand gay men infected/dead, before the president uttered the acronym.
Ashes to ashes, dust-to-dust: Ronald Reagan, Rock Hudson.

Three decades later, I inhabit the closet no longer,
legally married, a mother.
A few men lived,
in their chests *I Will Survive.*
In the gay village, politicians court the vote,
butchy women in business suits mingle with
guileless boys and old activists who hand out safes.

TOLERANCE

Cat fears dog before they meet.
Soon dog lunges towards cat asleep.
Cat hisses, stands tall. Deluded dog
resumes chase 'til cat scratches its snout.

In time, dog may see the curve of tail
the yellow eyes, the stubby nose as cat,
not threat.
Cat too, may curl up closer to dog's sun-drenched fur
when there is no other warmth in the old house.

OUT OF THE BLUE

Blue diamonds sequin the brittle snow,
on a winter walk with dad and dog,
not long after I'd come out.

My father, who'd expressed nothing about it,
out of the blue says,
Well, you're in good company,
there are many famous people who were gay,
and he names them, has memorized them:
Oscar Wilde
W.H. Auden
Alexander The Great
Billie Holiday
Aristotle
Socrates
Vita Sackville West
Virginia Woolf

late afternoon sun glints across that Great Lake,
rays sparkle the diamond snow,
as warmth mounts and mantles my brow.

COME OUT

Stylized geometry,
pink triangle shadowed by black
above purple text—
Toronto's pride theme, 1993.

Come Out, urging,
statement—
it changes through years.
Some took offense,
mostly conservative men who had a lot to lose
but no, that's too simple.
There were women too, unwilling
to lose what little they had.

I was righteous, thought I had come out.
I'd told my high school friends, my parents, my aunt by then.
I celebrated in the streets with my friends,
eight of us in solid-coloured shirts,
walked in rainbow formation,
Made the cover of *Xtra*.
In my naïveté, I thought I was done.

Twenty years later, I'm still doing it,
the only thing I want to have come out of is my mother's womb.
Not to the kindergarten teacher, the triage nurse,
the dentist, the law clerk, the adoption worker,
or the posh woman in the condo elevator
who asks, *Which one of you is the mom?*
then turns to press any button she can
when I say, *We both are.*

The agent at the ticket counter,
glances at us with a question,
I nod before he gets the chance—
no words, but he understands.
Resignation passes over his face
with a raised eyebrow as if to say,
"When did this happen?"
I feign ignorance, glance at our kids, say,
"Follow Mama while Mom gets our bags checked."

It's like breathing, not birth.

A GAY CRÈCHE

Roy and Silo, two would-be dads
entwine their necks,
sit on their egg
until Tango is hatched.

And Tango Makes Three—
And Tango Makes...fundamentalists scared.
The book is widely banned.

But the awkward truth of animals can't be erased.
There are many more penguin mates—
Jumbs and Kermit, Z and Vielpnkt,
countless too in Asian zoos.

After seeing their mating behavior yield no results,
the Bremmer Zoo tested their pairs for infertility.
It turned out they had a gay crèche.
Aversion therapy failed.
After an outcry, the gay pairs were given eggs to hatch instead.

Of 8.7 million species,
even with observer bias,
500 are known to have homosexual relations—
primates to gut worms,
bison, brown rat,
caribou, koala, giraffe,
mallard, raccoon, emu.
Even the fruit fly, desert tortoise,
box crab, raven,
wood turtle, bean weevil, barn owl,
orca, glasswing butterfly,
dolphin, ten-spined stickleback.

Without consideration for their researcher's ethical principles
or their theories of the biological drive to reproduce,
we prevail.
Maybe the Ark was the first gay cull—
left to drown in the flood
and yet, gay pairs persist
from the egg vents and abdominal flaps of their straight parents.

Roy tucks their baby girl in his brood patch,
while Silo finds food for his family.

BLOOD ORANGE

Joppa, Tarocco, Cara Cara, Sanguinello.
A hybrid between mandarin and pomello,
oranges grow near the Blood River in Limpopo,
alongside the ungraded dirt road, where the runners train,
barefoot, through the bush
in the red/orange co-mingle of sunrise,
in the descending crescendo of sunset.

After she shattered the 800 metre world record in Berlin,
Caster Semenya, of Limpopo, breathtakingly butch,
was accused of being a man,
jeered by the sixth and eighth place runners.
Deep voice, chiseled deltoids and biceps,
she visited the bathroom with competitors,
to show them her labia, again and again.

Her auntie says she knows what Caster is. She changed her nappies.
Turns out how we measure gender is complex.
No menses, not a big deal,
few female athletes bleed.
There is no definitive test.

She finds out she is intersex.
Undescended testes.
Mosaic female.

Caster retains the world record that she broke that night,
after the freak-show coverage and gender verification testing.
Hormone therapy renders her armour-like chest more curved,
her cheeks less angular, attenuates her power,
until we believe she is female.
Semenya goes on to win Olympic bronze, then gold.

Forget what you know.
Limpopo is South African slang for nowhere.

Imagine the dismay when you split one in half.
Red.
No, orange.
No, red.
There will be blood.

GONNA GET MARRIED

I can't marry you, my daughter's best friend declared.
I have to listen to my mom, and my mom says
I must marry a man.
But they are not women or men. They are five years old
and want to marry a different friend every week,
sometimes boys, sometimes girls.

Equal marriage rights passed ten years ago.
My daughter will not know of a time when her moms couldn't marry.
I must be sated with this; I must be sated with this
slow progress.

AMLAH, CLITORIS

Auto-correct transforms "amlah" into "and laugh."
Brilliant, I think.
I'm impressed until I type "l-a-b-i,"
trying to relay how my six-year-old twins
are comparing penis and labia.
But all I get is "labile."

For curiosity's sake, I type "c-l-i-t."
My device suggests "flit" and "Clinton."
Then I start to wonder if he's paid millions
for "ad placement."

We think them impartial—
those word prediction programs.

My son, Theo, says, "Yay! I'm going to have a twin brother,"
as they celebrate Franny growing a penis.
I say "no, that's her labia" to blank faces.
And they run in naked circles.

FORGIVENESS

*I wonder if that was how forgiveness budded; not with the fanfare of epiphany, but with
the pain gathering its things, packing up, and shipping away unannounced in the middle of
the night.*

— Khaled Hosseini, *The Kite Runner*

A drip that only smacks on the ceramic floor during torrents,
ignored
until the grout has split and gone soft,
though you tell yourself the tiles are impermeable.
One night as your wet soles slip
while scampering half-naked to the toilet,
you give in and put down a pail
after you tend your gashed knee.

You remember weeks later, only when it is brimming over
and start to dump it down the drain,
then reconsider and heft the container to the planter of parched lobelia
that you can never keep moist enough.

You ask them to forgive you
but they only flourish in their soil.

You think of your brother, unforgiveable, for gay-bashing you
and there begins a slant of light
(with its lure of release that is not nearly as inviting at midnight or noon)
into which context from the world pours.

BORN AGAIN

A family day together—
walk the dog, buy food and a leaf blower,
install storm windows,
play soccer on the sloping lawn,
eat pho in bowls and apples slathered in peanut butter,
cuddle in.
"Why does E.T. want to go home?
        Theo once asked if his tummy-mummy lives in outer space.
"Why are the scientists doing all those tests on E.T.?"
        The twins were poked and prodded, observed, subject to developmental tests,
"Is E.T. dying because he needs love?"
        Post-placement, they stopped developing while they attached.
        Franny said adoption was like being kidnapped.

After the movie, Theo says, "Can we play the born game?"
The two moms get on the floor,
while the twins crawl out, pretending to be just born.
The moms take turns catching and birthing them,
the twins alternate who is born first.
The moms hold them and say,
you are loved;
we will care for you
and we are a forever family.
The seven-year-olds, all brown eyes and hope, gaze at their mothers,
newly born.

THOUGH THE MILLS OF GOOD GRIND SLOWLY

Though the mills of God grind slowly; Yet they grind exceeding small;
Though with patience He stands waiting, With exactness grinds He all.

—Henry Wadsworth Longfellow

Everett Klippert, beloved
bus driver in 1960's Calgary,
charged with gross indecency, buggery.
His real crime is being gay.
No stand off or siege in a seedy bar.
The first time he pleads guilty to avoid headlines.

Klippert still serves ten years
but refuses his sentence of shame.
Yes, I had sex with men, yes,
I will do it again.

Arrest, admission, indefinite detention.
A declared "sex offender."
Supreme Court said so based on those archaic laws.
Even cowboy Calgary opposed a life sentence for consensual acts,
progressives thought it kinder
to call homosexuals mentally ill.

Then—Pierre Elliot Trudeau,
the state has no place in the bedrooms of the nation.

After release, Everett Klippert
drives truck up north, seeks solitude, freedom.
Never speaks of his roughing up in prison,
declined to be a gay spokesperson,
dies a darling brother and uncle in 1996.

In Canada, Stonewall is a town in Manitoba.
In America, Stonewall is a short for fight back.

Drag queens wearing women's underwear
were jailed for not conforming to their sex.
Whatever other courageous acts, living, loving openly,
mattered not
until, in 1969, the queens hurled Molotov cocktails and
bloodied their knuckles bare.
In America, you dare the state to kill you
or treat you fairly.

Everett refused to be shamed.
Though the mills of good grind slow,
they grind exceeding just
with exactness they grind all.

In 2016, Justin Trudeau granted Klippert a posthumous
pardon.

Bibliography

Andriote, John-Manuel. *Victory Deferred: How AIDS Changed Gay Life in America.* Chicago: University of Chicago Press, 1999.

Doty, Mark. *Heaven's Coast.* New York: HarperCollins, 1997.

Faderman, Lillian, *Odd Girls and Twilight Lovers: A History of Lesbian Life in Twentieth-Century America.* New York: Penguin Books, 1992.

Feinberg, Leslie. *Stone Butch Blues.* Ithaca: Firebrand Books, 1993.

France, David, and Joy Tomchin. *How to Survive a Plague.* Toronto: Public Square Films, 2012.

Hirshman, Linda. *Victory: The Triumphant Gay Revolution.* New York: Harper, 2012.

Lynch, Michael. *These Waves of Dying Friends.* Toronto: Contact II Publications, 1989.

Monette, Paul. *Borrowed Time: An AIDS Memoir.* New York: Houghton Mifflin Harcourt, 1998.

Shilts, Randy. *And the Band Played On: Politics, People, and the AIDS Epidemic.* New York: Stonewall Inn Editions , 2000 (first published 1987).

Silversides, Ann. *AIDS Activist: Michael Lynch and the Politics of Community.* Toronto: Between The Lines, 2003.

Weissman, David and Bill Weber. *We Were Here.* Weissman Projects, 2012.

Acknowledgements

I would like to thank the magazines and journals that first published these poems, sometimes in an earlier version:

Plenitude, Summer 2016, "What Lesbians Wear To The Mall"

Between The Lines, Spring 2016, "The Anita Bryant, A Gay Creche, March on Washington 1993, The Lavender Scare"

The Antigonish Review, upcoming Fall 2015, "Nothing To Forgive"

Plenitude, Spring 2014, "Where the Women Went"

Off The Rocks, edited by Allison Fradkin and published by NewTown Writers Press, Volume 18, 2014, "Come Out"

All my thanks to Banff Centre for the Arts, for the time and space to write. My deepest appreciation goes to Sharon McCartney for her keen eye, encouragement and shaping of the manuscript, to Arleen Paré for her careful reading, compassion and getting me unstuck near the end, to the Roombas poetry group for their sisterhood and many suggestions. As always, my deepest gratitude to my partner, Amy Bohigian for her encouragement, inspiration and close reading. Special thanks to Vici Johnstone, at Caitlin Press, for boldly and bravely starting a lesbian imprint. Special thanks to the LGBTQ communities of Nelson and Toronto, both of whom inspired and nurtured this work. I wish also to thank the Canadian Lesbian and Gay Archives and the GLBT History Museum in San Francisco.

About the Author

Jane Byers lives with her wife and two children in Nelson, British Columbia. She writes about human resilience in the context of raising children, lesbian and gay issues, and health and safety in the workplace. She has worked as an ergonomist and vocational rehabilitation consultant for many years and is passionate about facilitating resilience in ill and injured workers. She has had poems, essays and short fiction published in a variety of books and literary magazines in Canada, the US and the UK, including *Grain, Rattle, Descant,* the *Antigonish Review,* the *Canadian Journal of Hockey Literature, Our Times, Poetry in Transit* and *Best Canadian Poetry 2014.* Her first book of poetry, *Steeling Effects,* was published by Caitlin Press in 2014.

About the Cover Artist

Suzo Hickey is a painter and multidisciplinary artist. She graduated from Emily Carr College of Art and Design in 1994 and has exhibited around BC and the US on themes of queer mothering, urban landscapes, and death in the family. Her work has always been informed by the specifics of her life: the death of her twenty-four-year old son in *Mirificus,* stereotyping and the reclamation of language in *You Fucking Fruit,* and being a queer mother in *Let Me Go Down in the Mud.*

Recently, Suzo's work has been urban landscape. After constructing many shows around issues, she began examining the formal, non-verbal, enigmatic power of what was around her: the ordinariness of rainy intersections and leafless trees in her East Vancouver neighbourhood. After twenty-five years in Vancouver, she has moved back to Prince Rupert, where she grew up. She can be found online at her website www.suzohickey.ca.